Quotism

A collection of frank and humorous statements made by secondary school pupils on the autistic spectrum

Martin Howarth-Hynes Snr.

Published by Martin Howarth-Hynes Snr.

Publishing partner: Paragon Publishing, Rothersthorpe

ISBN 978-1-78222-906-3

Front cover: Martin Howarth-Hynes Snr.

Book design, layout and production management by Into Print
www.intoprint.net
+44 (0)1604 832149

Dedicated to Patricia Lomax.
The lead teacher at two of the ASD bases that I have worked
at. The most professional, caring, understanding and generous
person I know. A true friend.

"The man who moves a mountain begins by carrying away small stones."

— *Confucius*

Abbreviations

TA... Teaching Assistant

ASD...Autistic Spectrum Disorder Autism is a lifelong developmental disability. This affects how people with ASD communicate and interact with the world.

ADHD...Attention Deficit Hyperactivity Disorder Attention deficit hyperactivity disorder is a condition that affects people's behaviour. People with ADHD can seem restless, may have trouble concentrating and may act on impulse.

Quotism

In these pages you will, hopefully, be able to share and understand the sometimes sharp, witty and most of all, honest comments made by secondary school pupils that are on the autistic spectrum. These comments have been quickly jotted down and collected over a period of four years.

I have worked with these pupils one to one in mainstream (the main school) also in the ASD base, which is a set of classrooms set aside from the main school with an aim to help the pupils with ASD to eventually become more independent, build up confidence, self-esteem and most important of all, to learn the social skills that they will need in what seems to them a strange and sometimes frightening world.

What strikes me more working with these pupils is their honesty. It can be cutting, nobody likes to hear bad things about themselves, even if it is the truth. The pupils don't mean to offend, they are just saying what they think, which could get them into trouble. So, one of our tasks was to help them to learn what might offend and what could be OK to say. This was done mostly in social skills lessons, using role play, which the pupils loved. This was an important lesson that would help them on their journey through our strange world of sound, idioms, facial expressions, tone of voice etc... All these things that seem so 'normal', so natural to us, are hard to understand for a person with ASD.

So, here is a brief insight along their journey.

The pupils' names have been changed.

James

We start with James. James was a large, jolly and helpful boy. He watched a lot of American shows on TV, mainly cartoons. He would copy their speech and so would speak with an American accent. So, when you read his quotes, think American.

Computers

On seeing the computers for the first time in the ASD base, James turned to the lead teacher and in a low American drawl he exclaimed with disgust...

"Old monitor, new console, bad combination."

Pupils with ASD don't like change. It can make them anxious and upset. So, whenever there was a change: classroom, teacher, timetable etc., pupils would be notified. On this day James had a different teacher for a maths lesson. James was notified and he went reluctantly to the classroom. On his return a he was asked by another pupil what his new teacher was like. James answered...

"She's got a hard smile."

"What do you mean?"

"I mean I don't trust her."

On moving to France

"My parents are thinking of moving to France, but I want to stay in merry old England!"

Talking about films

"I warn you, if you haven't seen the modern version of Frankenstein before, well, it's not for the squeamish or the faint *haunted!*"

Most school children don't like homework. Pupils with ASD find it particularly difficult to understand why they have to do it. School is school were school work should be done. Home is where you chill out and do what you want to do, which is nothing to do with school. This is what we heard from most of our pupils in the ASD base. So, time was set aside so they could complete their 'homework' in one of the classrooms in the base. This worked really well and the pupils were less anxious and angry, and with help, they usually completed all homework on time.

On his homework

"I came, I saw, I *shall* complete this work!"

Sex education

In this lesson the class were acting out certain scenarios, and had to show the class what was the right thing to do and what was wrong. They would then have a discussion about it. James quickly volunteered to take part; he liked acting and was later to be in the school production of *Bugsy Malone* which you will hear more about later. Anyway, James had to pretend to be stood on a street corner with a friend, a young lady would walk past them; what would be the right thing to do? This was James' response in a loud American accent...

"Look at the size of those mogoomalas!"

*A lesson, I think, on **not** to say.*

PE

James came hurriedly back from PE in a state of distress, we soon found out why...

"I've been hit in the family jewels!"

James was chatting to another pupil in the ASD base about PE. "I don't like PE because I keep being hit by the ball," exclaimed the pupil. James thought about this for a moment, then answered...

"Yes, it's especially bad below the waist, below the waist is a bad place for balls."

Toilet

On using the toilet in the ASD base, James stormed out and announced...

"This toilet smells of old pee!"

James came back from a lesson and was quite pleased with himself.

"We've been working in there like Japanese monkeys!"

Sneezing in lesson

"What the hell, I've got snot on my tie!"

In art

When taking a suspected hair out of his artwork, which actually was a part of his paintbrush...

"My eyelashes are molting quite a lot lately."

Watching the film *Ace Ventura.*

In the ASD base at lunchtime, there was a choice of watching a film. The pupils would take turns to choose a film, on this occasion it was James' turn.

He chose *Ace Ventura.*

"What on earth is he eating?"

"Bat poo."

"Yuk, he doesn't know where it's been!"

Waiting

James, when in the classroom wanted to start working straight away. So, he was a little impatient waiting for the other pupils to enter the room.

"Come in, come in, while we're still young!"

Alton Towers

James loved theme parks. He was getting excited as the time of the reward trip to Alton Towers was looming. The reward trip was a school day out at a theme park for those pupils who had worked hard, had good behaviour and attendance. James fitted all the criteria.

"This time next month I will be on the ride 'air.' I will be laughing like a hyena on steroids!"

I asked James who the student outside the ASD base was waiting for…

"You get no prizes for guessing who he's waiting for."

He answered a bit like John Wayne.

"Who's he waiting for then?"

"I don't know."

RE

In the lesson they were discussing fasting and what is meant by using control. When asked the question, James' hand shot up in the air.

"I know exactly what that means, because on the way to holiday, I had drunk too much juice while driving to Holland. I had to wait seven hours

before going to the toilet, and what a relief that was!"

Rival

James tried to get on with everyone, but there was one pupil he didn't like at all, this was John and the feeling was mutual. They were both quick witted and always had a clever answer for everything. They would always try to outdo each other and no matter how hard we tried, they would never be civil to each other. So, we tried to keep them apart or kept a close eye on them when they were together.

James' old rival had forgotten his lunch.

"He can keep his hands off my lunchbox!"

If John was there, he would have had an answer to that I'm sure.

As James was walking up to the ASD base, he happened to see John through the fire exit window in the dark. John found it difficult to sleep and would come in school very tired. So, he was set aside some time to be in the base where it was quite and he could relax and rest, re-charge his batteries until he was ready for school work. This worked, it was useless to send him to lessons before he was ready. He would be anxious, angry emotional or just put his head on the table and ignore all requests to pay attention and begin his task. Of course, James did not care or understand about this, he just thought John was, as usual, being lazy. So, when he saw John in the dark, he had a grumble…

"Who the hell does he think he is, sitting there in the dark, a vampire?"

Competition Time

James started to have an obsession with entering competitions. He would bring in magazines and newspapers and show us the ones he had entered, mostly with computer games or consoles as prizes. This obsession however, did not last long, as he wasn't winning anything. At the time of his obsession he happened to notice an advertisement in a newspaper that one of the TAs had brought in. On seeing that it was a competition, his eyes lit up and with a loud exited voice he announced…

"Oh, my bleeding heart. Win an X box 360, I'm definitely entering that one!"

At the end of each lesson a bell would sound. James was hard at work and wanted it completed. So, as everyone was starting to pack up…

"This lesson aint over till the fat bell rings!"

The school show and a 'crush'

James was to be in the school production of *Bugsy Malone*. Amongst other things, he was to sing a song with a girl we shall call Jane. James had a crush on this girl and the feeling seemed to be mutual. However, Jane announced that she would be dressed, for some unknown reason, as Katy Price. James knew who Katy Price was and wasn't impressed at all.

"Jane dressed as Katy price is a disgusting thought to me!"

When asked why? He answered…

"I'm not going to directly tell you, but all I'll say is, as long as our act doesn't involve trying to make our private parts bigger, that's OK with me. That's all I'm saying, and that's that!"

Some confusion there. So, after a short chat about body parts, how they work and who has what, James was a little more forgiving about *his* Katy Price.

After a very successful show, in which James proved to be a very capable actor, and being pleased with his and Jane's performance, he was now happily packing up his things ready for home…

"Well that's two things I've got sorted out this afternoon: My love life and … my bag."

The next day I was joking with James, telling him not to leave the ASD base as there were crowds of girls outside, who had seen the show and might want to kiss him. He answered in an unconcerned American accent…

"That won't happen, I haven't brushed my teeth for two weeks."

I said *"Yuk, James, that's disgusting!"*

"Well actually, it was a week."

That's OK then!

Food Tech

On being told by another pupil, who was working with James, that he would be busy getting the equipment ready. James quipped…

"Busy, like a Japanese beaver possessed on steroids!"

Science

James had just finished drawing one of the planets of the solar system. He looked up and asked:

"What's next?"

"Uranus" was the answer.
James spun around on his chair.

"You what?" he gasped with a giggle.

The teacher began to explain about the seventh planet from the sun, but it was too late; James and the rest of the class, to the annoyance of the teacher, were in fits of laughter.

John

John had many things that he had to cope with: his Autism, ADHD, emotional and problems at home, he found it hard to sleep, which I have mentioned earlier, and on top of all this, he had to somehow concentrate on his school work. It is no wonder he was sometimes grumpy!

John was the king of Putdowns; he could be quite scathing in his comments but also very witty. This was, I think, Johns way of keeping people at a distance. He only had a select few who he would permit to encroach into his private world, and even then, they did not escape his cutting criticism. And yet he could be very caring and helpful, (although he would never admit to it.) I have witnessed him on several occasions helping pupils in the ASD base with their work. John was very intelligent and surprisingly knowledgeable about many things. Which brought him into conflict with James. John did not like James at all, and the feeling was precipitated. James would challenge John on a statement that he had made, and an argument would be inevitable. It was usual for them to try and outdo each other with cutting and witty comments at every opportunity. This was one thing that they both enjoyed and I'm afraid, that is how it stayed, until they parted company five years later at the end of year eleven. So, here are some quotes from John…

CATs

In year seven, all pupils have to do a test on their thinking with words, thinking with numbers and thinking with shape and space. This is called a CATs test. This was John's comment on hearing that he had to do one.

"Who needs a CATs test? I need a CAT scan!"

John had sensitive hearing, which was part of his ASD, so noise was a problem. This was his comment after coming back, rather disgruntled, from a geography lesson.

"My God, that teacher hasn't half got a loud voice for an old guy!"

John had sat through most of the lesson with his hands covering his ears.

Rivals

The old rivals, John and James. James not happy about John telling him what to do.

James... **"The day I take orders from you, a monkey will crawl outa my khyber!"**

John... "Find me a monkey!"

Who won that one?

A question on John's RE exam paper:
'Do you believe in sex before marriage?'
John wrote...

"I'm a fifteen-year-old boy, what do you think?"

In RE they were reading a story set in 1890. It was about a man who loved three women and couldn't decide which one to marry. John was asked by the teacher 'how should he decide?'
(I braced myself)

"They could mud wrestle"

came his reply, quite matter of factly. The teacher, after quietening the rest of the class down, persisted *(he should have known better)* 'What if he couldn't decide from this?' he asked. John smiled. This was a smile that I recognized, a smile that showed he was going in for the 'killer' blow. After a moment of anticipation from the whole class, he answered...

"Topless boxing."

The teacher, giving up, quickly moved on.

PE

John found PE the most difficult of lessons. If outside, John found it too hot, too bright (on a few occasions he had worn my sunglasses) or too cold. He didn't like the feel of the PE kit and he could not wear trainers, for he had, on top of everything else, an on-going, in-growing toenail. This made John, at times, even grumpier. His elevated grumpiness was a sure sign that a PE lesson was looming. In the end, to spare him the misery, it was decided that it was in John's interest for him not to do PE. So, when he was asked by a teacher why he didn't do PE, he simply said...

"I don't do PE because I haven't any suitable footwear"...

And that, was that.

On reminding John, he had five minutes left to finish his work:

"Hey, five minutes left for me?"

(He was good at sarcasm.)

"Yes," I said. "If you're good."

"Well, I haven't killed you yet, so, that's good enough."

On being told that the headmistress had turned a failing school around:

"Yes, turned it into the fourth Reich!"

Overhearing the TA in the next room, helping with some history...

TA... "Photographs are a good source of evidence."

John... "Yes, and they are a good source of blackmail too!"

Word search

I said: "I'm no good at word search."
John replied:

"Neither am I, get over it!"

John was given some sweets for his good work. When asked if he was going to share them, his reply was...

"No, I'm selfish, remember."

"There's a fine line between healthy eating and communism."

The work of Charles Dickens

The teacher asked John to give his opinion on how Oliver Twist was treated. John, without an ounce of sympathy replied...

"I think he bloody well deserved it. Next question."

Tony

Tony, apart from his autism, was a very angry young man. He struggled to understand the day to day things that we, as non autistic people, just take for granted. He couldn't share things that belonged to him, he didn't like to share his ideas about his school work, in case someone "stole them." And he did not like losing, be it a board game, cards, computer game etc. So, PE was a big problem. He could not accept the other team getting more points than his, and he would become abusive to the point where he had to be taken out of the lesson, away from the other pupils. He would be taken to the ASD base where he could be quiet and slowly helped to calm down. When he was eventually settled, things could be calmly explained to him: why the other team did this, why it is OK to lose, why it is not OK to respond the way he did. Of course, at first, he didn't agree with the explanations given. But over time he learned to become more tolerant, less angry and less confrontational with his peers. This was the case with Tony saying what he thought about people, no matter who they were. He would just say it to their face. Most things that he would utter were not flattering, but more derogatory. This was a dangerous thing for him to be doing in a mainstream secondary school. So, through social skills group and role play (which he wasn't too keen on) he slowly began to mostly 'think it, but not say it.' The role plays really helped him to distinguish between the right and wrong things to say. This helped him to get along with his peers in and outside the ASD base, and set him up for his journey through college life and life in general.

Here are a few gems from Tony.

On describing his headache…

"Hey, my brains bursting!"

On being told that he had to go to PE with a TA who he had previously called the "Frankenstein monster" *(should have just thought that)*, he replied…

"I'm not going anywhere with the living dead!"

And when playing the 'tell me' game in the social skills group, Tony was asked the question: What 'S' is a language?

"Do I have to say it?"

"Yes."

"Shit" he replied, ecstatic at being allowed to swear.

Tony had misunderstood the meaning of language and a word. His thought was language is words and it is, but he could not grasp the concept, at first, that what was meant was a foreign language such as Switzerland, not words that make up languages, hence his reply.

Tony's cat

"I've got a cat called Harry; I call him Ginger no nuts."

"Why do you call him that?"

He was asked by an unsuspecting TA, who immediately wished that they hadn't.

"Because, he's been castrated. He's called Ginger pubes as well."

Tony was impulsive, full of surprises and at times, very funny. One example is, when we were walking back from a lesson, Tony suddenly asked…

"Have you ever done that dance, like this?"

He then folded his arms and proceeded to attempt a Russian Cossack dance.

"Oh, I said, do you mean that Russian dance?"

"Yeah, can you do it?"

"Of course, I can." *(I lied)*

"Well," he began, **"I tried it and nearly split my testicles in half!"**

Without another word, we quickly moved on to the next lesson.

Paul

Paul had high functioning autism. One of the effects of this is that his language skills were not as developed as they should. So, at times Tony found it difficult to express himself verbally. Saying that, he did get by in school pretty well. Everyone liked Paul. He was very choosey who he would speak to. He had to trust and feel comfortable with that person and this often took a long time. I was very honoured and privileged to be to be in Paul's 'circle of trust'. We got along really well; he liked my sense of humour and I liked his honesty.

Paul was a strong young man but had a gentle nature. People saw this and that is why, I think, they liked him so much. One of the things he was passionate about was: protecting women from being hit by men. "Men should not hit women!" He was always ready to come to their rescue.

As I have said, everyone liked Paul and would 'look out for him'; this made Paul feel safe in the school environment and less stressed.

This was most evident in PE. The other pupils would look after him, when they were choosing teams for football for instance, they would make sure Paul wasn't picked last. They would always pass him the ball, even though it might end up anywhere except where it was intended to. He was included in everything, and made to feel that he was the same as them and not different.

One day, there was a new boy in PE. On seeing Paul, he began to make fun of the way he was running. Paul thought it was a bit of fun and was putting up with it. As the boy carried on I could see Paul was becoming anxious, so, I was about to intervene. I had no need to. Immediately the other boys turned on the new boy and warned him off. The boy apologized to Paul and that was the end of the matter. I noticed that in the next PE lesson, this boy was as helpful to Paul as the rest of the class.

So, here are a few 'gems' from Paul.

Whistling

I like whistling, but when at school I was respectful of the pupils (and adults) in ASD base who did not appreciate my high pitch renditions of current popular music. So, I tried not to whistle when at school. Paul did not like to hear anyone whistling. One afternoon whilst in the base, I had a relapse and began to whistle. I was in about ten seconds of the tune when Paul shouted from the other room…

"Shut the noise up, moron!"

That put me in my place.

Science

I showed Paul a picture of a man who had been buried under the ice for five thousand years. Paul said...

"Bloody hell, I bet he's dead by now."

Curry

We were chatting about curry, I said that I liked mild curry. Paul said...

"You're not a man until you've had a Vindaloo."

Which brings me to the time when I was with Paul on his work experience. I was with him for one week at a garage where MOTs on large vehicles were performed. Paul was interested in the workings of the combustion engine and cars in general. He did well at the garage, the people who Paul were working with were very good with Paul. They let him help them at quiet moments and on things we knew that he could cope with. I mostly kept my distance and let him get on with it, only intervening when I had recognized that there might be a problem.

When you work with a pupil you become aware of: the things that make them happy; the things that make them sad; what will stress them out and what they will need help with the most. And most crucially, to recognize when to intervene before they get stressed. An example of this with Paul was when we went for our lunch at a local Chinese takeaway.

As I have said before Paul loved a curry. So a trip to the Chinese takeaway seemed a good idea. When we got there I ordered my chips and curry straight away, but Paul was taking a long time to choose his meal. Then I realized that Paul always went to the same takeaway near where he lived. Also, he knew it by choosing a number, the numbered meals in this takeaway did not correspond to the ones in his local one and there were so many other options. I could tell he was becoming anxious and he would not know how to explain to the person serving behind the counter what the problem was. So, I said to Paul quickly and calmly, "Do you want the same as me?" He said "Yes" just as quickly, and I could see the relief on his face. So, in the end we had a good dinner and Paul carried on happily with the rest of the day.

Playing cards

Paul and I used to play cards every lunch time. The same time, the same game, the same cards. But it was never boring. We played a game we called twenty-one or pontoon.

One day someone had changed the cards with some larger ones; they were three times as big as our usual ones. This was Paul's response as he shuffled them…

"Look at the size of these bitches!"

Ancestors

Whilst discussing his ancestry, Paul decided that he was half Viking, this was partly because he had blonde hair. He then stated that he…

"Couldn't speak *Vikish*."

Gender

"A boy dressed up as a girl, he's *Tri sexual!*"

Not being intentionally sexist, just saying it as he saw it. Paul did not fully understand why a boy would want to be a girl and vice versa. To him a man should be a man and a woman should be a woman. And men should be the ones to protect women.

In social skills lessons he was taught that this is not always the case, and why someone might feel the way they do about their gender, and want to change.

Keith

Keith was a quiet boy who loved dinosaurs. He would be constantly drawing them at every spare moment. He would make his own comic strips, which would tell a good, witty and exiting story.

Keith had ASD and was very literal and honest with his comments. Here are just a few of his spontaneous responses…

Having a cold

Coming back to the ASD base mid-lesson. Keith walked slowly into the base classroom and announced…

"I'm a little bit ill, if you want you can look up my nose and see the snot."

We declined the offer.

End of term

Keith opened the door to the ASD base and – to his surprise and apparent disgust – saw three TAs celebrating end of term and dancing to that well-known party ditty: 'Agadoo'. Keith strode into the room and said, quite bluntly…

"I have some advice for you… Grow up!"

Some *good* advice there.

The ASD base is a quiet and calm place for pupils on the spectrum to be, when they are feeling upset or a little ill, and need to be in the calmness away from the sometimes noisy and busy main school. Sometimes they may have time to finish off their 'homework'. This is what Keith was doing, when suddenly a girl let out a screech as she passed the base windows.

This was Keith's startled response…

"God, I didn't see that coming; her shouting like that, she jumped me well bad!"

Robert

Robert was a boy struggling with his autism. He was finding the world even stranger as he became a teenager. Puberty can be a strange thing for most young people, but for someone on the autistic spectrum it can be a frightening prospect. There are a lot of changes going on, changes that you have no control over, and to most autistic people change is very frightening.

So, these are a few misconceptions Robert had about sex, which fortunately, he was not shy about asking.

Robert said that he knew how a man and woman had sex...

"You see, a man puts his willy into a ladies tuppence, but does the lady ever go to the toilet again, and does the man get his willy back?"

He was told not to worry. The lady would indeed be able to go to the toilet again and the man would certainly get his willy back. Robert, as you can understand, was very relieved.

On another occasion, Robert was chatting to another pupil and asked him...

"What's it called when you get that funny feeling in your willy?"

The other student thought for a moment, then replied...

"I think it's anorexia."

Robert asked a male TA in the ASD base...

"When you put a condom on your willy to stop sperm escaping, does it still feel nice?"

The TA, taken aback by this sudden and somewhat personal question, quickly spluttered his answer...
"Yes," he said.
Robert, satisfied with the answer, carried on working. There was however, to the embarrassment of the TA, some muffled giggles emanating from the other classroom.

Stuart

Stuart, a boy on the autistic spectrum, who struggled to understand the concept of Christianity. RE lessons baffled him and although he did the work that he was asked to do, he didn't see the point in it.

To him this world was complicated enough without having to learn or believe in another.

So, in his RE exam, he got his revenge...

RE

A question on Stuart's RE exam paper:

'Why do Christians believe Easter is more important than Christmas?'

Stuarts answer...

"Because they always look on the dull side of things."

Another RE exam question:

Two bullies keep poking fun at Mark. The teachers don't help. Joey is a good boxer and is tempted to sort out the two bullies. What should he do?

Stuart's answer...

"Give Joey two knuckle busters and tell him to get on with it!"

Kyle

This complicated world would sometimes make Kyle very angry. He would lash out (verbally) to shock and say things that he didn't really mean. He would sometimes get himself into a situation that he found hard to get out of. And not being able to explain his predicament, he became even angrier. We, who worked with Kyle, knew what things could make him anxious and angry and usually saw the problem before it happened and were able to, mostly make Kyle's journey through school a smooth one. Things that could make him anxious, and others, were: if there was a different teacher; a change of classroom; not understanding the class work. These are just some of the things that could make Kyle anxious. His anxiety was lessened by notifying him of these changes. Also, social skills group in the ASD base helped him to manage his anger and cope with the anxieties of school life. Happily, when he left school and started college, he had become a much less angry person. He was the happy person that *he* wanted to be, and that *we* wanted him to be.

Anyway, here are some of the thing Kyle would say in his *angry* times…

"I'm going to blow up this school!"

"But I'll be here, and I'll get blown up too."

"OK, I'll do it when you're on a course."

Going to Maths

"I wish I was dead!"

"What would I do then Kyle? I wouldn't have anyone to go to maths with."

"Well you'd find some other kid to go with you wouldn't you!"

Kyle was asked: 'Who are the Queen's grandchildren?' Kyle grumpily answered…

"I don't know do I? I don't live in London!"

Liam

Liam was a very pleasant, timid, quiet boy. He was on the autistic spectrum and in the first years of secondary school he wouldn't speak much. He would answer when someone spoke to him, but would never instigate a conversation. One day, whilst still in year seven, we went down to the PE department and informed by the other boys that they were going to do football. Liam on hearing this became upset and started to well up. I found out that he was scared of the ball hitting him, having, I learned, been hit in the face with one at primary school.

So, I asked the teacher if Liam could do something else. I knew Liam liked running, so it was decided that, instead of football, he could do as many laps around the tennis court as he wanted. It was wonderful to see how happy this made Liam. Sometimes I would run with him, but he was in charge, this was *his* thing, something he was good at (especially in PE) and that made all the difference. The other pupils would always cheer him on, not mockingly but wanting him to succeed. This was a great boost for his self-esteem and to his delight his nickname (again not mockingly) from then on was Forest Gump. Football would have made his life a misery.

Sometimes, between running, we would play a gentle game of catch the ball. Or practise throwing the ball in the net on the basketball court. Just to lessen the fear of the dreaded ball.

Not until year 9 did Liam begin to join in conversations confidently. This was due to the hard work in social skills group; work done by the lady who did speech and language therapy; the amazing teacher in charge and the team of dedicated TAs in the ASD base. Liam became more confident and began to be more talkative and … funny. Also, the girls liked him, which was a mystery to Liam, but he liked the attention. He was easy to like. He was good natured, kind and never said a bad word about anybody.

Liam didn't understand verbal jokes, but he did enjoy practical jokes especially when he was the perpetrator. He would sneak toy spiders into school in order to frighten a certain TA he knew didn't like them. *The TA really didn't like them!* Liam didn't, *couldn't* understand how his joke spiders frightened the TA so much. So, in social skills he was shown how upset the TA might feel. I used the example of how he felt when he was told he was going to do football in PE. This must have worked because this is what he said to the same TA whilst in his art lesson.

"I'm going on my computer tonight and getting pictures of spiders. Brace yourself miss, they're not that scary, they're nice."

Afterword

So this ends my brief but wonderful journey into the world of pupils with ASD and ADHD.

I would like to add that gaining the trust and respect with both fellow TAs and pupils is very important. Also to be honest and trustworthy. As regards fellow TAs, it is essential to share knowledge about a pupil that they are working with; if another TA is finding it difficult to motivate a pupil then sharing the way they have dealt with a certain situation might help. Being consistent is less confusing for the pupil and TAs working as a team is essential.

Also, and I think this is even more important, a TA has to have bags and bags of patience!

In 2021 I retired (early) and the pupils that are mentioned must now be in their twenties and thirties. All went on to college and are living as 'normal' a life as possible. It can't be easy, but hopefully their time in the ASD base has given them the tools to cope socially and confidently in this complicated world.

FURTHER INFORMATION

National Autistic Society

393 City Road

London

EC1V 1NG

Tel: +44(0)2078332299

Email: nas@nas.org.uk

National Autistic Society Scotland

Clockwise

7th Floor

77 Renfrew Street

Glasgow

G2 3BZ

Tel: +44(0)141 221 8090

Email: scotland@nas.org.uk

National Autistic Society Cymru

2nd Floor

Lancaster House

106 Maes-y-Coed Road

Heath

Cardiff

CF14 4HE

Tel: +44(0)2920 629 312

Email: Wales@nas.org.uk

National Autistic Society NI Autism Centre

East Bank House

East Bank Road

Carryduff

Castlereagh

N Ireland

BT88BD

Tel : +44(0)2890 687 066

Email: northern.ireland@nas.org.uk

Child Autism Helpline

01344 882248

Autism NHS

www.nhs.uk

Autism/Aspergers-Supportline

www.addiss.co